Unbroken

By
Tonia A Strickland

DEDICATION

This book is a dedication to my dad for allowing me to take care
of him as long as I could.

Love and miss you, Daddy.

TABLE OF CONTENTS

CHAPTER 1

The beginning of my life as a little girl is blurry. I don't remember much, but I was told that my birth mother had me and didn't want me. She even lied to my dad, saying I belonged to another man, a claim I find deeply disrespectful. On top of that, she had another child, my brother, and didn't want him either. We were placed in separate foster homes.

Meanwhile, she went on to have two more children, and this time, she kept them. That truth cut me deeply.

What kind of woman does that? She was an alcoholic, but even that is no excuse for giving up her first two children. The mother of four, yet only keeping half. For me, it was devastating. I grew up heartless in many ways because I never knew what a mother's love felt like. She robbed me of that, stole it from me, and left me to grow up in pain.

As a child, that reality ruined me. Over time, I built up a lot of hatred toward this woman. When people refer to her as my mom, I correct them. She's not my mom. A real mother doesn't give her children away and then go on to have more and keep them.

My grandmother, the only mom I ever knew, was the one who found us. The story I was told is that she spoke with God, asking Him to help her find her grandbabies. God led her to me, and though it was harder to find my brother, He showed her where to go. When she discovered us, I was walking, and my brother was crawling.

My dad signed over his rights to his mother, and so she became our mom. Sadly, I had to be adopted because of the lies my birth mother had told him. But in truth, it was a blessing to have someone who went out of her way to find her babies. On our birth certificates, her name was listed instead of that so-called woman.

This beautiful lady gave us the best she could. Even when she struggled, we always had food, clothes, shoes, and a roof over our heads. She wasn't my biological mother, but she was the only mother I knew. She even told me that when she found me, I was already calling her "mom." From that moment on, everyone let me continue calling her mom, and I always did.

CHAPTER 2

As I got older, I began to realize what people were saying about that so-called woman. The more my mom explained, the more I told her how much I hated her. My mom would just tell me, "Let God deal with it. Stop saying those things."

When it came to my brother, though, whatever he did was always okay with my mom. I remember once he took her car without permission. Instead of punishing him, she hurried to call her son, who came and let my brother drive the van. I asked if I could drive too, but of course, the answer was no.

Then there was the time he and a friend decided to hide out in the mall until closing. They got caught and ended up in jail. My mom even told the cops, "If you've got him, keep him. Don't bring him back home."

Eventually, his friend's mother, who used to date my dad, went downtown and bailed them both out. Later that night, my brother came knocking at the door. My mom warned me, "Don't you dare open that door." But what did I do? I opened it. I got cussed out so bad. She said, "Didn't I tell you not to open the door? That's exactly what I meant!" And sure enough, my brother got his butt whipped after that.

She said, "What the heck were you thinking? You thought you weren't going to get caught? What was the plan, change into different clothes and walk out of the mall like you had just gotten there?" Then she told him, "You've got to be the stupidest child I've ever seen."

She pressed him further, "So if I told you to jump off a bridge, you'd do it? Then she said back to him, "Then why did you both stay in the mall?" He had nothing to say, just stood there looking foolish. I teased him, "Guess you're not the good child after all."

But despite all of that, he and I had a tight bond. As my mom used to say, we were like two peas in a pod. If my brother did something wrong and I knew about it, I wouldn't snitch, unless we got mad at each other. Then the truth would come out.

I remember one time when we went to the store, and my mom warned us: "Don't touch anything. Don't ask for anything." We promised, "Okay, Mom." But my brother still stole a watch. When she found out, she marched him back into the store, made him return it, and told him, "I'm going to whoop you."

Another time, we went into a different store, and this time, I was the one who decided to steal. I took some nail polish, thinking I had a straight shot. But I forgot about the floor vent. She smelled it, called me downstairs, made me hold out my hands, and tore me up badly. When I say this woman didn't play, I mean it, she didn't play.

When it came to fighting, my brother was the type to start a fight and finish it. If he even heard I was about to fight, it was already over. Once, the oldest sister wanted to fight me. I don't know how my brother found out, but he gave that girl a black eye. He was truly my best friend. We shared secrets no one else ever knew.

I remember so much about him, what he did, what he didn't do. But in my daddy's eyes, he never did anything wrong. One day, he was waiting for me to come home, sitting on the banister. It broke, and he cut his hand on some glass, slicing his main artery. Blood poured out like water. My mom rushed him to the hospital, and the doctors confirmed the artery was cut. They stitched him up.

To this day, I still can't stand the sight of blood. I remember when it came to my brother, I could never catch a break with my dad. It was always, "My brother this, my brother that." One day, he made me so mad that I started teasing him about the way he used to talk. Right away, my mom jumped in: "Stop teasing him."

Later, my mom decided to put us in a Catholic school. I knew it wasn't for me. I told her straight up, "This school isn't for us. We're not Catholic, so why are we going here?" I thought I was about to get smacked for saying that, but instead she just said, "You're going, and that's it."

We didn't last long in that school anyway. The breaking point came when a nun slapped my brother. That was it. I turned to my mom and said, "See? I told you we weren't going to be here long."

Not long after, my mom moved out of town with her son and his wife. For me, that was rough. It felt like suddenly I had a stepmom telling me what to do. I already had a mom in my life; I didn't need another woman stepping in. As a teenager, it was just too much to handle.

It was a lot for me to take in, trying to deal with everything going on in my life. I still couldn't get over the fact that my birth mother had literally given me away, and now I had a stepmom trying to be a mom to me when she didn't even know how to dress me or buy me shoes. Nobody really paid attention to my behavior.

One day, down in the basement by myself, I wrote a suicide letter and left it on the table. I don't even know who found it. All I know is that my dad ended up making an appointment for me to see a therapist. That didn't go well. I refused to talk to a stranger, especially with my dad sitting right there in the room. I just twirled around in the chair, and he got pissed. But what did they expect? I was a teenager.

When my stepmom got pregnant, all hell broke loose for me. Suddenly, I had to deal with a crying baby sister and even less attention on me. So, I started doing what teenagers do, skipping school. Nobody knew, because I made sure I showed up for the first hour. After that, I'd go over to my friend's house when she skipped too, since her mom would be at work.

Before school was out, I would sneak off and pretend like I'd gone to class. I thought I had everybody fooled, but my mom knew. Eventually, I got in trouble.

Not long after, my mom decided she was ready to move back home, and I went with her. I couldn't wait to get back, but once I did, things spiraled out of control. "Out of control" doesn't even begin to describe it.

One day, I stayed out all night and didn't come home. My mom was furious. She even called the police, but they couldn't find me. When I finally came back, she called her son to come over and lecture me. I wasn't trying to hear it. He told me, "You say you don't have a mom, well, then you don't have a dad either." I just shrugged and said, "That's fine by me."

I felt like nobody cared about me anyway. So, I packed up my stuff and left. I never spoke to my dad again, not until years later, when I got pregnant with my son. She told her son that, "I had a son." And when asked who the baby looked like, the answer came: "He looks just like your daughter."

CHAPTER 3:

TRUST AND MOTHERHOOD

When it came to trust, there was only one person I could count on, my mom. She was the one I was around the most, the one I confided in about everything.

When I became pregnant again, I didn't even have to tell her. She already knew. My dad, on the other hand, wasn't happy at all. Of course, he gave me one of his lectures. But I didn't care. I was grown, living on my own, and taking care of my responsibilities without their help.

Yes, I was on assistance, but I was also working while raising my two children. It didn't bother me that their dads weren't involved. I was strong enough to be both mom and dad, holding down the home and caring for my kids.

Things got complicated when my third child came along. That's when it got a little ugly. With this pregnancy, it became a guessing game. I wasn't sure for a moment, but deep down, I did know. Both men were tested, and I knew it wasn't the first man's baby. My mom, though, wanted it to be, because she didn't like the other guy.

My dad tried to deny one of my kids, saying, "That's not his baby." I told him, "Yes, it is." Sometimes when you're dealing with parents, all you can do is shake your head.

When I sit back and think about it, I realize how differently I treated my kids compared to the way the woman who birthed me treated hers. Never in a million years would I consider giving my kids up for adoption.

I'll admit, at one point, my stepmom wanted custody of my oldest son, and I let her have temporary custody. But he was still family, and he wasn't a little baby. By the time he was 8, he was back with me. I loved my kids. They were spoiled as hell, and I never treated one differently from the other. Whether it was shoes, clothes, phones, or anything else, I made sure they all had what they needed.

My youngest son, though, was always getting sick or running a fever. One night, he had an asthma attack and a fever at the same time. It was strange, at night he would struggle, but during the day he'd be fine. His dad offered to take him to his appointment to find out what was going on. I agreed and went to work that morning. On the way, his dad called me and said they were heading to the doctor. I told him, "Stay in touch and let me know what the doctor says."

My boss came to me and said I needed to head to the hospital right away, they were about to do emergency surgery on my child. No details were given, just that I had to get there. I drove as fast as I could, praying I'd make it, and thankfully, I arrived just in time before they put him under.

The doctors explained that the surgery went well. They found a tumor that had been cutting off his airway. He was heavily sedated, and they told me to go home, eat, rest, and come back in the morning. But I couldn't bring myself to leave my baby in the children's ICU.

When I returned the next day, I broke down. Seeing him with all those tubes and wires hooked up to him was more than I could take. He didn't even know we were there. He stayed in the ICU for five days before he was finally able to go home. When he was discharged, the doctors gave us a list of what he could and couldn't eat. The very first thing he reached for was a slice of bologna. It was like nothing had ever bothered him.

When school started for him, it was just him and his Big Mom at home, since the older two were already in school. They would tease, saying, "Big Mom spoils him, and he gets away with everything." And honestly, he did.

"Well, you know that's her baby," people would say. He was the only one who stayed home with her while the other two were off at school. Honestly, I didn't mind.

By the time my kids were older, we spent more time going to the mall, a hotel just to get away, or even bowling. We were always doing something different, so they never really stayed home much.

Birthdays were always special, too. I made sure of it. My kids had things a lot of other kids didn't, and people used to tell me, "Your kids are so spoiled." And you know what? They were, and I was proud of that. They were mine, and I was going to spoil them. My mom had a hand in that, too. These days, what kid isn't spoiled? Even animals are spoiled.

My last child, though, he was her baby all day long. Even his dad admitted it. Once everyone knew I was having a boy, everything changed. My mom was there for every single one of my childbirths, and that meant the world to me. She always made my day just by being there. I love that woman so much.

CHAPTER 4:

LOSING MY HEART

When my oldest kid was a teenager and the other two were still young, I got a call from my dad. He asked where everybody was and what we were doing. I kept asking him, "Why? What's going on?" But he wouldn't say. He waited until the kids were gone before finally telling me.

When my kids came home, they talked to their granddad, but still no one told me what was happening. At last, my dad broke the news: my grandmother, my mom, had passed away.

I dropped the phone, screaming and crying, "No! No! No!" She was my heart, the love of my life. The thought of her being gone made me so angry. I kept asking myself, "Who am I going to call now?"

The hardest part was preparing her funeral. Looking at caskets, writing her obituary, all of it broke me. She had made me her beneficiary instead of her son. That alone spoke volumes.

What haunts me most is the last time I saw her. I went to visit her at the nursing home, but she didn't even know who I was. Later, I learned she had been battling dementia for four years. No doctor had ever told me. Looking back, I believe she must have had Alzheimer's disease as well.

Losing my mom pushed me into a deep depression. One day at work, the lady I called my big sis slapped me across the face and said, "Come back, chick. You're about to end up in the psych ward, and I don't want to see you in the crazy hospital. Let's get back to the real world."

As the years passed after my mom's death, I tried to push forward. I bought a house for my kids and expanded my daycare so they had more room to grow. Work was going well, but eventually I got tired of running the daycare. Too many parents didn't want to pay or tried to take advantage, and it weighed heavily on me.

So, I gave it up and decided to go back into the field. Around the same time, I made another life-changing decision: I filed for divorce. I couldn't take the jealousy and insecurity anymore. My dad helped me with the first payment and the lawyer consultation.

The lawyer asked me, "Are you sure this is what you want?" I didn't hesitate. "Yes," I said. The paperwork was started, and once it was done, the papers were served to my husband.

He was mad as hell when he got served the divorce papers. I explained to him why, I couldn't take it anymore. I wasn't going to keep dealing with jealousy, insecurities, and constant arguing. Enough was enough.

It got so bad that I couldn't even take the kids to the hotel with my friend and her son for a simple outing. It was supposed to give them something different, a change of scenery. But he accused me of cheating and even tried to run us off the road in the snow. I thought, Who in their right mind would bring kids and a friend's child along to cheat? I wasn't a fool.

Then came the week when everything boiled over. I was at home, on the phone with my dad, when my husband came out, trying to figure out who I was talking to. I just looked at him and kept right on talking to my dad. He demanded, "You going to respond to me? If you want to talk to these men, go outside and talk."

I stayed put. Then he called me a "bopping ass bitch." I said to my dad, "Did you hear what he just called me?" My dad asked,

"What are you going to do?" And I answered, "I'm going to call my lawyer and bring in my last payment."

When the court date came, it was over quickly. As we sat in front of the judge, she turned to him and asked, "Do you have anything to say?" He shrugged and said, "I don't care to add anything. Just give her what she wants. I'm done."

The judge pressed him again: "Are you sure? What's your take on the marriage?" He refused to answer, simply saying, "I decline to speak on this." My lawyer had no more questions, and the judge granted my divorce, just like that. He grabbed his newspaper and phone and walked out of the courtroom.

Afterward, my depression and anxiety came roaring back. It was too much, losing my mom, going through a divorce, losing my job. I was under so much stress, and looking for another job only made it worse. Eventually, I found one that paid better, or at least I thought it would.

For a little while, it was steady. Then one day, the head owner came in and shut production down. The timing couldn't have been worse. I had just put money down on a house. It was crazy once again. I had to start all over, looking for work.

Chapter 5:

Starting Over

We were given servant's pay to help cover the rent, but I still had to look for work. During that time, I took in my daughter and grandson too, just until she could get back on her feet. When she finally found her own place, it was just me and my youngest son left in the house.

A couple of years later, I made the decision to pack up, give away some things, and leave town for good. My son's dad stayed behind in the house. I had a big reason for moving it was either my life or his, and I wasn't about to let a man push me to the point of ending up in jail. I've always stood firm on that. No man will ever play with my heart or my mind. Those were the kinds of games my husband tried to run on me, and I refuse to ever live like that again.

When I got to my brother's house, I settled in and felt some peace knowing things were good. The very next day, it was time to start looking for work. That wasn't easy because I didn't know the area well. But then I found out I had a friend nearby, and she pointed me toward some temp agencies. That connection put me back on track, and I finally started finding work again.

After searching and searching, I finally landed a good job. I stayed there for about a year and a half before switching to another position that paid a little more. I was determined to build my savings so I could eventually live on my own.

For a while, I continued living with my brother. During that time, he became seriously ill. As his big sister, I stepped in to take care of things. We found out he had a tumor in his head, which explained the headaches he'd been having. He went into surgery to have it removed, and while he recovered, I took care of the house and the dogs. Even after he came home, I made sure he was okay.

Not long after, our dad came to stay with us. That time brought me and him closer together. We bonded over father-daughter talks, play fights, and long conversations. Whenever I had questions about men, I went to my dad. I always felt like I could trust his answers, and he never steered me wrong. For some reason, I found it easier to go to him than to my brother. I don't know why, but it worked.

Eventually, I was ready to branch out. I left the nest, got my own apartment, and was loving the independence. But my dad wasn't too happy about it he didn't like my apartment...

I told my dad, "If you're able to talk, let them know your daughter is on her way. Give them my phone number." I wanted to make sure he was getting the right treatment.

He stayed in the hospital for a while before being transferred to rehab, where he began treatment for the left side of his body after a stroke. Those days weren't easy. More than once, I had to confront the CNAs because they weren't washing his clothes or changing him properly. Eventually, I started taking his clothes home to wash them myself and bringing them back.

People say caring for a parent is easy, but that was a lie. My dad was a handful, even giving the two physical therapists hell. He was an Army vet, and he loved talking about the Army. But it broke my heart to watch him go from walking to not walking at all.

One morning, I went downstairs to check on him and saw his eyes roll back in his head. I screamed, "Daddy, oh no, not on my watch!" I called 911, and they rushed him back to the hospital. I went to see him every single day.

Two weeks later, the hospital called. My dad had passed away.

CHAPTER 6:

SAYING GOODBYE

The hospital called and asked me to come view the body. I told them I'd be there as soon as I got dressed. When I arrived, the nurse walked me into the room and uncovered my daddy. The moment I saw him, I broke down, crying and saying, "My daddy is really gone."

The nurse quietly left the room, telling me she would give me a minute. I was grateful for that, because I needed the space to let it all out. I was hitting walls, asking God why He had to take my daddy.

Then came the paperwork, signing forms, making funeral arrangements, and choosing a funeral home. Thankfully, the lady helping me was very kind through it all.

But as always happens, when a family member passes, people start acting strange. Relatives who had nothing to do with him in life suddenly began demanding things, arguing over where, when, and how he should be buried. But I remembered what my daddy had said: "If I die where I am, that's where I want to be buried." That was his wish.

Still, the paperwork wasn't handled the way it should have been.

It seemed like everyone was more concerned with what they wanted to do with my dad than with honoring his wishes. To me, it felt like it was all about the money and who had control. Some even wanted to fly him back home and arrange a funeral there. I was furious. Nobody had taken care of him or been there for him while he was alive, and now, suddenly, they wanted to decide everything.

Two of his best friends called me, though, and gave me some peace of mind. They told me that even though my dad wasn't always easy to understand, they knew what he wanted. He had made it clear that if he ever got sick, he wanted his oldest child, who was me, to take care of him.

Hearing that made me proud. I was the chosen one. And I believe it's because I never asked him for anything. I always got things on my own. I never needed a man to take care of me either, because I knew it would just be thrown back in my face. I learned how to be independent.

That's how I raised myself to be the strong, self-sufficient woman, never begging a man to do for me what I could do for myself. My mom trained me well in that way. That doesn't mean a man can't do something for me, but I never depended on it. I've always paid my own bills and bought everything I needed for myself.

After losing two of the most important people in my life, depression and anxiety began to take over. I didn't know if I was coming or going. Eventually, I walked into a facility seeking help for my depression, anxiety, and stress. While I was there, I also sought a second opinion about my fainting spells, or syncope.

They scheduled me for a tilt table test. They strapped me down, then tilted the table upright. Within ten minutes, my heart rate and blood pressure dropped. To test further, they placed nitroglycerin oil under my tongue and told me to let it dissolve.

The next thing I knew, I felt dizzy and asked to be lowered back down. After that, I don't remember anything. When I finally came to, the doctors explained that they'd struggled to bring me back, and it scared them. I was exhausted. They asked if I had ever felt like that before, and I told them no. That's when the doctor explained that what I had experienced was neurocardiogenic syncope and warned me that it could come back again.

CHAPTER 7:

A LIFE SCARE

Living with syncope and vertigo has changed my life, but nothing prepared me for what happened when COVID-19 first hit. I experienced vertigo so severe that it felt like something I had never gone through before. I couldn't stand up on my own. If I leaned to the left, the whole room would spin. Even simple things, like washing myself, became impossible.

Eventually, I had to text for help just to get to the bathroom. The spinning was relentless. It got so bad that someone had to call 911. When the paramedics arrived, they checked my blood pressure, my temperature, and asked about my medications. Then they asked if I could sit up or stand on my own. I told them no and the fear in my voice was real. This wasn't normal for me at all.

To make matters worse, because of COVID restrictions, no one was allowed to go with me to the hospital. I felt completely alone. At the hospital, they ran test after test, asking endless questions. I grew frustrated and started going off on the doctors. I kept telling them, "I can't sit up or stand on my own!" But instead of listening, they seemed irritated with me. Their frustration only fueled mine. I was scared, angry, and feeling abandoned, knowing nobody could be by my side.

At the hospital, I couldn't understand why all this was happening to me. At one point, the doctor even had the nerve to say, "We can send you back home." I told him flat out, "If I go back home, I'll just end up right back here. It makes no sense to send me home."

So, they admitted me into the hospital. I stayed for a while, and before I could be discharged, the nurse made me walk around to prove I was strong enough to go home. I did, but once I got back home, I still had to take it easy. They weren't confident that I was in the clear.

The truth was, they didn't know what triggered the vertigo, just like they never figured out what caused the syncope. But what I did know was this: I would never be able to work the way I wanted to again. Between the syncope, the migraines, and now the carpal tunnel, so many of the things I once loved to do were no longer possible.

The doctors scheduled me for surgery to implant a loop recorder, a device that monitors the heart, to see if I was having seizures in my sleep. They suspected that might be the case, but nobody really knew for sure. What I did know was that standing for more than twenty minutes could cause serious problems, and that was enough to change my life.

When the doctors asked me about my family history, I told them there wasn't much I could share. I didn't know everything about my family's medical background, especially on my biological mother's side. I had no idea if her family was alive or gone, let alone what health issues they might have had.

On my daddy's side, I knew there was high blood pressure and strokes, but beyond that, not much else. So, when it came to figuring out where my syncope came from, there were no answers. The vertigo, I was told, likely came from my dad's side, but thankfully, I didn't carry all of his symptoms.

Eventually, since I wasn't showing new symptoms of syncope, the doctors removed the loop recorder from my chest. Still, the combination of health issues made it nearly impossible for me to hold down a steady job. I remember when I first started working, they asked if I had any health problems. I told them about the carpal tunnel and migraine headaches. They gave me a sit-down job, but that didn't work out either; my hands started hurting too much.

Then, when I was officially diagnosed with syncope, the doctor told me straight: he was taking me off work for good.

CHAPTER 8:

FINDING JOY IN BAKING

Through everything I've been through, I've always worked, all kinds of jobs. I started out at KFC and Ponderosa, then moved on to factory jobs, working with transmission parts and operating machines. I worked for different companies, always keeping busy and earning my way.

Eventually, I decided to stay home and run a daycare. I got my home inspected for the food program, and before long, I was caring for children full-time. I loved the kids, they were never the problem. It was the parents who gave me trouble, not wanting to pay their co-pays, talking trash, and trying to drag my household down. But even with the challenges, I realized how much I missed working. It was part of who I was.

When health issues made it impossible for me to keep working, I found a new outlet: baking. What started as a way to pass the time became therapy for me. Baking filled a space in my heart that work once held. It brought me peace, and joy.

And it wasn't just for me. I loved seeing the smiles when people tasted what I made, knowing I put love into every dessert. From no-bake treats to two-layer cakes, pound cakes, cookies, cheesecakes, and more, I poured myself into it. I never thought I had baking skills, but I discovered that I did, and I did it well.

Baking became more than just a hobby for me it became a craft. Over time, I learned to come up with new ideas and create desserts from scratch. Sometimes people would send me a picture of a cake and ask, "Can you make this?" I'd smile and say, "Yes, let me check what I need." Then I'd turn on some music, step into the kitchen, and make magic happen.

But I had rules. If someone called and asked, "Can I get a cake tomorrow?" I had to tell them no. Baking from scratch isn't like grabbing a box mix. I couldn't just throw together cold ingredients and expect it to come out right. My cakes were real, made with patience and love.

Some people were surprised. "Oh, I didn't know. I'm just used to box cakes." I'd reassure them, "That's okay. Not everyone knows the difference, unless they're a baker."

I even tried to pass the skill on. Once, I asked a friend if she wanted to learn. She laughed and said, "I'll leave the baking to you." I still remember her coming over while I was making a pound cake. She pulled out her phone to record me, and I told her, "Don't just record, come on and learn the game of baking."

CHAPTER 9:

LOSING MY BROTHER

Even though I loved spending time in the kitchen, baking and cooking, life had a way of interrupting with moments I wasn't ready for. One particular day, I received a phone call. For some reason, people always start those conversations with, "What are you doing? Are you sitting down?" I never understood that.

This time, it was my sister. I asked her why she was calling like that, and she broke the news: my brother was dead.

I couldn't believe it. I told her no, that couldn't be true. She said she was on her way to me, and I told her fine, I wasn't going anywhere. When she arrived, I was already feeling torn up inside. The last time I had seen him was when my stepmom had passed away. My sister said, "Let's go get a drink to calm your nerves." We did, but even afterward, coming back home, I was still messed up from it all.

This wasn't just any brother. This was my blood brother, from the same mom and dad. Losing him felt like losing my best friend. He had always had my back, from when we were kids all the way up into adulthood. We were like two peas in a pod, and I always said he was the crazy one of the bunch.

Now, with him gone, my sister and I had to meet with my niece to figure out what needed to be done and what had happened to him.

It was a heavy burden on my niece, the same one I had carried when my dad passed. She had to gather information, break the news to the family, and somehow face the truth herself. She went to the funeral home, saw the body, handled the arrangements, and prepared the obituary. It's work that tears at your heart, because no matter how much you do, nothing can bring him back.

When I look at my brother's daughter, it feels like looking straight at him. She has his same deep dimples, even his walk reminds me of him. Every time I see her, I'm reminded of how much I miss him, how much I miss my brother my best friend.

People don't understand what it feels like to lose a sibling unless they've walked in those same shoes. Now I have nobody. My three beautiful angels my mom, my dad, and my brother are all gone, together. When I say my world is turned upside down, I mean it with every piece of me.

I can't call my mom. I can't talk to my dad. I can't see my brother's face pop up on social media. It feels unreal. These days, I lean on my other brothers for answers, or my sister, or even my best friend, who has become like a sister. She's always there for me, and I never forget to tell her thank you.

CHAPTER 10

This is what makes me see the world differently. The things I've been through in my life feel unbelievable, and even now, I still struggle to come to terms with it all. I often ask myself how I can keep going, knowing that so many of the people I once loved are no longer here. I cared for my mom, my grandma, and my daddy's son, and yet now I feel numb inside. Sometimes I open up about it, but most times I don't. Especially when people only ask to be nosey. They act concerned, but I know it's not real concern; it's just something for them to repeat, twisting my story into something else.

My mom used to remind me, "Everybody isn't your friend," and she never lied about that. I had to learn the hard way, but it's still a lesson worth carrying. People say lessons learned are blessings, and I believe that. She also told me never to be a butt-kisser, never to lose myself just to please others.

They say a mother always knows best, and she never steered me wrong. Family has always been everything to me, and my siblings remain deeply important to who I am.

Life has its challenges. It can take you from the highest of highs to the lowest of lows in the blink of an eye. I've lived through every moment of it, my health struggles, jobs, family, the b.s., and the heartbreak of losing loved ones.

It's been one hell of a ride. I've escaped near-death situations with buses, cars, and other close calls I never thought I'd survive. Each time, all I could do was look up and thank God. Without Him, where would I be?

When I look back, I think about the person I used to be, someone who thought abuse was love. I endured every kind of abuse: mental, physical, emotional. I took it until one day I woke up and said, "Enough is enough." That was the turning point.

Now, as an older woman, I don't tolerate lies, cheating, games, drama, disloyalty, or lack of communication. Those are dealbreakers.

My abuse was brutal. I was punched in the face, stomach, and ribs. I was dragged down stairs, my face shoved into a sink full of water, my hair ripped out. But I survived. And survival has given me a new standard: I know what I will never go back to again.

My head was slammed against the shower door. I was dragged outside in the freezing snow by my hair or my jacket. I was young and dumb, and I thought I had to take it.

But ladies, listen when we're young, we put up with too much of men's b.s. As we grow older, enough is enough. If men aren't hitting us, they're killing us.

Ladies! Ladies! Ladies! For your safety, get out. Stay out of abusive relationships or marriages. We are not punching bags. We are not here to be beaten down. We must love ourselves first. We must put God first.

I had to learn self-love the hard way. I had to love myself before I could ever let someone else love me. Now, every time I look in the mirror, I remind myself: *I am a woman. I am beautiful.*

I tell young women this all the time: do not let yourself become some man's punching bag. God did not put us on this earth to be abused, belittled, or treated like we're worth nothing. Men who act this way are not men at all they're little boys.

A real man treats a woman the way he treats and loves his mama. But some will never know how to do that.

CHAPTER 11

The only person I did not mention is my favorite. This lady means the world to me. She is the love of my life. When we talk, we talk about everything.

I wish I had a close bond with my uncle, but I always talked to her. Before my dad passed and still to this day, I talk to her. My dad and his sister were really close. Any time I came around and heard him on the phone, I would ask, "Who are you talking to?" He would say, "I am talking to my sister." And I would ask why, and then say, "Because I am being nosey, that is all."

I do not remember if he had a close bond with his brother before. You would have thought my dad and his sister were the only two siblings. They had another brother who passed away before my dad ever got sick. Now that my dad has passed, it is only my uncle and my aunt.

I remember when I was young. My granddad was so drunk that night. I was trying to help my granddad's wife down the steps, and she fell. When he found out, he was ready to shoot and kill.

That is how it felt to grow up around all of this. I kept close to the people who made me feel safe, and she was that person for me. Even now, when I do not have the words for what I am feeling, she listens. She never rushes me, never judges me, and somehow she always knows how to calm my heart. I think that is why my dad stayed so close to his sister too. In a family where tempers could explode and old pain sat just under the skin, her voice was steady. She was the one who made space for the truth.

CHAPTER 12

When it comes to my siblings, we share the same dad, but we have different moms. Still, no matter what or how we grew up, we have some type of bond. Some of us lost our moms, and we lost a brother. He was my blood brother by the same mother.

But way before my brother passed, I found out that my birth mom had passed too. And the truth is, I did not have any real remorse for this woman. I just said, "Oh wow. What did she die from?" They told me cancer. I said, "Oh, okay." That was it. There was no emotion, no tears, no deep ache in my chest. It was just a fact to me, like being told the weather outside.

When I finally met this woman, I did not even know what to call her. Everyone else might have thought I should call her "mom," but it did not feel right to me. So, I just called her by her name. That's what felt natural. That's what I could live with. I figured if my heart didn't recognize her as my mother, why should my mouth?

I knew deep down that the person who raised me was more important than she ever was. Blood may connect people, but love is what makes a parent. And she had never given me that love. I often think about how much more I value the ones who actually showed up for me, the ones who fed me, cared for me, taught me lessons, and stood beside me when life got hard. That mattered more than anything a title could give.

Like they say, you have to forgive yourself for the things that do not make sense to you. For a long time, I questioned myself—why didn't I feel sad when she passed? Why didn't I cry, even a little? But the truth is, you can't miss what you never really had. You can't mourn someone who was never there to begin with.

So, tell me this: how would you feel? I am a grown woman, and I still cannot come to grips with all of this. I still wrestle with the idea that the woman who gave birth to me also gave up on me. I wonder sometimes if I carry pieces of her in me—her habits, her ways of thinking, maybe even her weaknesses. But then I remind myself, I am not her. My life is my own.

Even now, though, there's a small ache inside. Not grief, but a kind of emptiness. It's the unanswered questions, the things I'll never get to ask her, and the words I'll never hear from her. Maybe that's what makes it harder—the not knowing. Did she ever think about me when she was gone? Did she ever regret the choices she made? Did she ever, even once, wish she had been different?

I'll never know. And maybe I don't need to know. What I do know is that family is not always about blood—it's about love, sacrifice, and presence. And that's what I hold on to when I think about her, about my siblings, and about the family I chose for myself.

CHAPTER 13

This chapter is solely based on things that matter to me and to other people out here in the real world. We deal with them on a daily basis. The system has failed some children in foster care, where they don't check on these kids like they are supposed to.

My brother and I still don't really know how we ended up in foster care. To this day, I don't have the answer. But somehow, we were placed in different homes, separated from each other. And yet, for us, I guess you could say we were blessed to have a grandmother who truly cared and loved us as if we were her own babies.

The children out here now are not so lucky. They're being abused, neglected, beaten, or even killed—sometimes by family members, sometimes by total strangers. I think about that a lot, and I realize just how fragile a child's safety really is.

The crazy thing is, I never got to ask my birth mom why she did what she did. I never asked her why she gave us up. And on top of that, she lied about my dad not being my dad. It was like she was a monster, hiding the truth from us, and I never knew anything real about her. From what I was told, her family was dead, but I never tried to find them or figure out where they stayed. I guess part of me didn't care. And if they were still living, why did they let this happen to my brother and myself?

My dad's mom used to say a lot about this woman, but I never knew whether to believe her or not. She once told me, "If you want to know, just go downtown and find out the things you want to know about her." But I didn't ask questions. I stayed quiet, because everyone who could've answered is now gone.

Thinking back, from being a child to a teenager, from a young adult to now being an adult woman, I realize I still carry all these issues. They never really left me. Therapy didn't fix it. Silence didn't erase it. And pretending to be okay only made the pain worse. So what are you supposed to do when you've already sought help, but the help didn't work?

People don't matter to me the way they used to. I don't care if it's family or friends. Everybody wants to talk, wants to judge, wants to ask questions and twist your answers into something you never said, just to make themselves look good. That's why I always say: you can't really believe people. Because when they get confronted, they'll lie. They'll always lie about things they don't want to face.

Still, I think about the children coming up now. Children sitting in foster care, wondering why their parents left them, asking themselves if they did something wrong. I know that pain. I lived that pain. And I want them to know that even though the system fails, even though people lie, even though family can abandon you—your story doesn't have to end there.

What matters is finding your own truth, creating your own family, and never letting the lies of others define who you are.

CHAPTER 14

My love life was like searching for love in all the wrong places. Every time I thought I'd found love, it turned out to be something else entirely.

I tried again and again. One man I stayed with for quite some time, hoping things would last. But hope wasn't enough. With him came the cheating and the lies. He'd beg me, "Please forgive me. I won't do it again." I gave him chance after chance, but he couldn't stop. Eventually, I let go. I told him, "You just can't help yourself. You want to have your cake and eat it too." Not on my watch.

When I moved out of town, I met another man. At first, he seemed perfect cool, responsible, everything I thought a man was supposed to be. But that illusion faded quick. He hated paying bills, spent his money on women, and filled my ears with lies.

Still, I tried again. We even got a marriage license. The plan was to go back out of town, get married, and start fresh together. But before that could happen, he cheated on me. This time, I didn't hesitate. I told him, "I'm so glad I didn't go through with the marriage."

He swore up and down that he "didn't do anything." But of course, he kept trying to come back over and over again. Years later, he'd still call me, asking the same questions: "Can we get married? I miss you."

And I'd tell him straight: "How can you miss me, let alone love me, when you never really wanted me? After everything I did for you and you still dogged me who does that? Oh yeah, you did."

My time is valuable. I refuse to let anyone waste it. Some people love to play with your heart, and then, when it all falls apart, they want to cry like they're the victim. No you don't get to play the victim when you caused the problem.

The truth is, when people play with your heart, they don't realize the damage it can do. Hearts break and sometimes broken hearts make people snap. Lives get lost. And nobody, nobody, should ever have to go through that ordeal.

CHAPTER 15

Raising my three young adults and now watching them raise children of their own has been a blessing. I came a long way as a single mom, and I loved every bit of it. Some of these young mothers today need to learn to stand on their own two feet, instead of leaning on men who don't want to step up and be fathers.

I learned that lesson with my first child. From the start, I told myself I would never depend on anyone else to do for my baby what I could do myself. I bought what my child needed, and when his father complained to my mother about me spending too much, she told him straight: "It's her first child. If she wants to buy him $200 worth of clothes and toys, then she can." He didn't like it, but I didn't care. That was *our* child, and I was going to take care of him.

By the time my second child came along, things were a little different. Her father stepped up more, made sure to be present, and even took her to stay with him some nights. Sometimes she stayed with her grandparents, too. But most of the time, she was right there with me. And like my first, she was spoiled with love.

The youngest of my children was definitely the spoiled one, though I never played favorites among them. I loved each of my children equally. But when it comes to my grandchildren, I'll admit I have my favorites, and so did their granddad. His favorites were the youngest three, while mine were the oldest two and the very youngest. Still, I wouldn't trade or change a single one of them. I love all my grandbabies with my whole heart.

I like to tease them sometimes. I'll pick up one of my granddaughters and say, "You're not my favorite your sister is." She'll pout, roll her eyes, or get mad, and I just laugh. That's the joy of being a grandmother you get to play, tease, and love in your own way.

With my youngest son, things are different but just as special. We go back and forth, sometimes arguing, sometimes laughing. He'll get mad at me, or I'll get mad at him, but our bond never breaks. Once he cools off, he thinks about what he said or did, apologizes, and then we're right back to joking. My daughter is the same way. I don't sugarcoat things for my grown kids. I treat them the same way I treat the grandkids if they're wrong, I tell them they're wrong. That honesty keeps us close.

I've never been one to sugarcoat things. I'm straightforward with all of them kids, grandkids, whoever. If they don't like what I say, that's their problem. I mean what I say, and I don't back down.

My grandkids especially know this about me. I don't play with them. I tell them, "I didn't take backtalk from your mom or dad, and I'm not taking it from you." They get the message quick, even if it means they don't like coming around as much. I know I can be strict, but when I'm serious, I'm serious. I don't play with a smart mouth.

My son's daughter stays with him, and my daughter's boys come around sometimes. Other than that, I keep my peace and don't bother with anyone unless I have to.

My youngest son likes to joke that I'm a grandma and should stay home. I tell him, "No, I don't. I stay home because I choose to." I like to travel, I like to get out of town when I can. Still, if he calls me to pick up the kids from school, I'll do it. That's what family is for.

CHAPTER 16

Rebuilding my bond with my daughter has been priceless. We've come a long way from clashing daily to growing into a relationship that feels more like mother and friend. Back then, we bumped heads constantly. I was always the babysitter, the one stepping in when she wanted to go out or work.

But her baby boy? He was my baby too. I'd been there from day one. If he cried while she was sleeping, I'd scoop him up, change him, and feed him. She'd get upset, but I didn't care. I wasn't about to let him cry when I could help.

Sometimes I cooked, sometimes she did. If I made breakfast, she'd make dinner. And though we argued plenty, one thing was clear: she doesn't play about me. Being her only girl, she always knew she could lean on me or on her dad. I remind her now, "You're not a little kid anymore. It's time for you to take care of me."

I once asked her, "When I get old, what will you do? Put me in a nursing home?" She looked at me and said, "No, I'm going to take care of you." And I believed her.

He never corrected them, never set the record straight. He just went with the flow. But for me, there was no confusion. We were just friends, and that's all we would ever be. Once I'm done, I'm done. There's no going back.

I told him plain and clear I would never get back with him. No marriage. No girlfriend title. Nothing. I remember once, after I had surgery, he asked me if I would marry him again. I hung up the phone and said no. When he asked why I couldn't at least think about it, I told him, "There's nothing to think about. I know what we've been through, and I'm not going through it again."

I give my all in a relationship, but if someone takes that for granted, they don't get another chance with me. I believe in treating a man like a king, and I expect to be treated like a queen in return. That's fair. But the moment disrespect enters the picture that's the moment I cut ties for good.

CHAPTER 17

After nine and a half years, I chose to stay single. I had grown tired of men and their unbelievable stories, their empty promises that I couldn't trust as far as I could throw. In all the relationships I had, I never found serious love. At best, they lasted three to five years before I started falling out of love because there was no love left to feel.

I would hear the same tired words: *"I love you, you know I'd do anything for you."* But the reality was different. There was no trust. No loyalty. And without those things, words mean nothing.

So I would go silent. I wouldn't even announce the end of the relationship. I would simply disappear, go ghost. Eventually, the phone would ring, and the man on the other end would ask, *"What's going on?"*

I'd tell them, *"You figure it out. I've been done. You just didn't see the signs. I was pulling back, talking less. That was your answer."*

If a man couldn't give me what I needed, I decided I didn't need him at all. Still, I kept running into men who claimed they wanted a relationship but proved otherwise. Eventually, I grew exhausted with the cycle. And so I quit.

CHAPTER 18

I thank God for allowing me to write this book my story, my truth, and the things I've lived through as a child.

There are pieces of my early years I don't remember, and sometimes that absence hurts more than the memories. But there is one thing I was told: as a baby, a woman burned me with a hot comb. Maybe that was why people labeled me a crybaby. Maybe that was why we were put into foster care. The truth about my childhood died with the people who could have told me.

Because of that, I understand the pain of children being taken from their parents and placed in foster care. But here's the truth foster care doesn't always mean better care. Some foster parents were no better than the biological parents those children were removed from.

Still, not all foster parents were the same. Some truly loved the children they took in, and it wasn't about the money. To them, it was about giving love. I tip my hat to those good ones. I've seen both sides with my own eyes: children who were well dressed, cared for, and loved and others who looked like nobody cared at all.

The system has to do better. Children deserve more. I often wonder if they took me and my brother, why didn't they take my other two siblings away from that woman as well? It's something I still can't come to grips with. Even now, I struggle to call her my mother, because in my heart, she was no mother to me.

How can a woman who once told me she didn't know why God allowed my brother to be born ever deserve the name "mother"? What kind of woman speaks that way about her own child? What kind of woman has children only to abuse them?

The treatment we endured was beyond cruel. I still ask myself: What did we do so wrong to deserve it? Where was the love we should have known? The truth is, the pain of that question will haunt me for the rest of my life.

But I also recognize something powerful. I thank God for the gift of grandmothers and grandfathers who step in to raise their grandchildren with love, patience, and sacrifice. Not every child gets that blessing. Some children are raised in homes where parents are lost in drugs, alcohol, or selfish neglect, leaving the kids to fend for themselves. Some children are forced to raise themselves while still living under the same roof as their parents.

I wasn't blessed with a loving mother, but I can appreciate and honor those who do step up, who choose love when others do not.

In my opinion, too many people have children for all the wrong reasons just to collect food stamps or government assistance without truly caring for those little lives they've brought into the world. You can see it plain as day: the parents walking around well-dressed, hair done, looking sharp, while their children look neglected. It makes you stop and wonder, *What is really going on here?*

For me, it was the opposite. My kids always came first. I made sure they were dressed well, their hair done, their needs met even if it meant I went without. I would go broke for myself before I let them go without. My children never wanted for anything; they had it all.

People used to tell me, "You've spoiled your kids." Maybe I did, but I don't see it that way. To me, I was simply giving them the love, care, and stability I never had. My kids had things many children didn't get to have, and I don't say that to brag. I say it because I am proud of the way I poured everything I had into raising them.

CHAPTER 19

Well, well, let's talk about men. How is it that men always say they want a long-term relationship, but when you give them just that, everything starts off smooth until the silence comes? Suddenly, communication stops, and when they finally surface again, they've got a story ready. Some excuse about why they weren't talking to you. And the thing is, it's never just once. It becomes a pattern.

When you ask them where the relationship is going, they'll say, *"Oh, we're going to make this work, we're going to continue."* And because your heart is invested, because you trust them, you agree. You trust them especially because you've already shared your past, you've told them about the hurt you don't want to repeat.

But when that trust is broken, things can get very ugly. If you hurt my heart, if you hurt my feelings, that's not something I take lightly. Sometimes I think, *Men really be trying me.* Because the truth is, lies can ruin someone's whole life. And for what? I don't need karma showing up at my door. The funny thing is, the more you lie, the more tangled the lies get.

The truth always comes out. And it's often that one person you never would've expected who turns on you especially someone you thought had your back for years. At first, you don't want to believe what another woman tells you. But then you start asking questions about what you've done for the man, or what the inside of his house looks like. That's when you realize she has no reason to lie.

The real kicker is when you finally call him, and instead of facing you, he ignores your calls, your texts, and even your video calls. There's no need to hide the truth is already out. The only thing left to do is apologize for the lies and deceit.

But notice how when a woman does the same thing, it suddenly becomes a bigger problem. Men are quick to call us every name in the book. They'll kick us out of the house, and if we're married, they'll divorce us. Still, a fake relationship isn't worth holding onto. There's no need to explain yourself just pack your things and leave.

This world is truly messed up. Too many people refuse to take accountability for their actions.

I've learned to always be honest with someone before getting involved. Let them know what you have going on, and then leave the decision up to them if they want to continue. It's better to tell the truth from the start than to go into a relationship full of lies, because eventually those lies pile up and the truth comes out.

For me personally, I'd rather hear the truth and decide for myself if I still want to talk to you or if it's best we just remain friends. But once my feelings get invested and I find out you've been lying, there's going to be hell to pay. Trust me. Just keep it real with me, and we'll be good. I don't want my heart or my emotions to be played with.

And if you can't even be man enough to tell me how you really feel or admit when you're wrong, then you were never for me. From now on, I'll keep my heart guarded until God brings me the right man.

CHAPTER 20

This is my new life, my fresh beginning. From now on, I'm focusing on myself instead of pouring all my energy into everyone else. For so long, I put others before me just to make them happy, but the same effort was rarely returned. Still, I did it out of loyalty to friends, to family, and even in relationships.

But now, I'm choosing me. No more unnecessary stress. No more draining myself to keep others satisfied. I'm giving myself something I should've given long ago: **self-love.**

I once spoke to a woman who told me something powerful: *"You can't please everybody. You'll never get back everything you put out."* She said you'll eventually see people's true colors right before your eyes. And when that happens, you'll question yourself *What did I do wrong?* But the truth is, it's not you, it's them. Once they've taken everything they can, they'll kick you to the curb and talk behind your back.

She was right. I wish I had gotten her name and number, to tell her how much her words stayed with me. I've always valued the wisdom of older people, because they've lived it. They've been through it. And their knowledge is priceless.

I've always loved listening to the older generation talk about their experiences what they've endured, what they've overcome. As you sit and listen, you find yourself thinking, *Wow, I'm going through that right now… or I just went through that.* Their wisdom hits different when life proves it true.

I've learned so much from my mom, my grandmother, and my aunt. And what I didn't learn from them, I learned on my own through struggles, through mistakes, through pain. I've been through a lot of crap, but that's life. You live, you learn, and you grow.

Now I take time to sit back and reflect. I think about what I need to change within myself and what I need to stop tolerating. I've learned not to let people walk all over me.

These days, when I look in the mirror, I remind myself: *You are a beautiful woman. You love yourself. It's time to turn your life around.* I refuse to settle for less. I've learned to stand strong, to set boundaries, because people won't respect you if you don't. Too often, they make everything about themselves, and it's never about you. And the moment you make it about you, they get mad.

Whether I'm at home or away, my mind is always in motion, always thinking about my next move. But after dealing with so much nonsense, I know it's time for a real change in my life. God is taking the wheel now, guiding me in the direction I need to go.

Because let's be real too many men are out here playing childish games. Not all of them, of course, and not all women either. But here's the truth: if you have a good man, hold on to him. And gentlemen, if you have a good woman, cherish her.

The sad reality is that some people don't even love themselves, so how could they truly love someone else? You can give them everything your time, your heart, your love but if they don't know how to return it, you'll always be left empty.

That's why now, when I meet men, I keep my guard up and my heart shielded. I refuse to let another soul hurt me, play with my emotions, or drag me into drama I don't deserve. I'll never again allow a man's girlfriend or wife to call my phone like I'm the problem, when the truth is, he's the one lying.

Women, stop blaming other women. Check your boyfriend. Check your husband. Because more often than not, they're the ones out here creating lies and drama.

People often ask me why I tell men exactly what I do for others or what others do for me. My answer is simple: it's better to be honest than to live a lie. Because once you start lying, the lies catch up with you. And eventually, you're left looking foolish.

I've been through that nonsense before, and I'm tired of it. Honestly, sometimes I'd rather be single than deal with childish boys who pretend to be men.

And I know I'm not the only one. I hear women talk about the same struggles all the time. Just like men sit around talking about what they don't like about women, we do the same thing pointing out what we don't like about them.

One time I was talking to a male friend about what I'd gone through with a certain man. He said he didn't really understand my situation, but I explained it to him anyway. And I made it clear this isn't about *all* men. Still, had done some of the very things I was describing. That's the point I was making: too many men can be so petty, sneaky, and secretive with their lies.

CHAPTER 21

I was on the phone with a good friend, opening up about my life. I told him my story, my history, and in that moment, I described myself as "damaged goods." Not because I'm broken, but because of everything I've been through from childhood to now.

People sometimes think I'm crazy, but the truth is, I'm not. I just don't have the patience for anyone's nonsense anymore, whether it's family, friends, or a relationship.

It feels like searching for love is a losing game. You meet a man, think he's perfect, give him your heart only to end up heartbroken when his true colors come out. And every time, I find myself asking: *What did I do to deserve this pain?*

I didn't grow up with my father around much, but when he was present, he taught me a few things about men. Still, no matter what I learned, relationships often start out good and then suddenly shift.

Sometimes I want to stay single, protect my peace, and focus only on me. But there are other times when I long for a relationship only, it has to be the right one. One built on love, honesty, and respect.

I've been single for nine years now. Why? Because too many men these days only want to lay up with you but don't want to do anything for you. They want the benefits free sex with nothing meaningful behind it.

This is why I say the world feels crazy sometimes. It's almost like you need to run a background check before dating a man, just to see if he's hiding something abuse, violence, instability, or worse. Some men come with too much baggage, and I refuse to let that into my life.

All I really want is simple: to find the right person to settle down with and grow old alongside. I'm not getting any younger, and like everyone else, I just want to be happy with someone who truly loves me.

I know I'll never find "Mr. Perfect" because I'm not perfect either. But at the very least, we should share real things in common beyond just the bedroom. Don't you agree?

Too many relationships and marriages these days turn into a mess. They end in divorce, or worse, in abuse where the man thinks an apology and a few gifts can erase the damage he's caused. But flowers and presents can't heal the scars left on your face, your body, or your heart.

Here's another thing I don't like: when you meet someone and the two of you are honest about what you like and don't like especially when it comes to communication. At first, he's calling and texting regularly, checking in, making it seem like he's consistent. But before long, the texts and calls start to fade. Suddenly, I'm the one reaching out, and I can't help but think, *What's going on here?*

Then come the excuses: *"I've been busy, I was going to return your call, what's the big deal?"* But the truth is, it feels like I'm the one chasing him. And I refuse to chase after a man.

So, I sit back and reflect on my life, wondering which direction it's headed. I don't want to grow old alone, but if I must, then so be it. I'd rather be at peace by myself than in a bad relationship with a man who acts like a boy.

And trust me, I've been down that road before. My ex-fiancé swore up and down that he was a man but in reality, he acted like nothing more than a little boy.

The more I think about dating again, the more it scares me. These days, it feels like there's no one you can truly trust. Too many men are either living double lives, manipulating, cheating, or lying.

I know, because I just went through it. I thought I had found the man of my dreams, but it all turned out to be a lie. And the worst part? He couldn't even come to me and apologize.

At first, everything felt perfect the connection, the vibe, the way things seemed to flow. But then everything came crashing down. The stress of it all even made me sick. I ended up having a syncope episode, blacking out, and barely remembering what had happened. What I do remember is what caused it.

I even texted him to let him know where I was, thinking he'd show some care or concern. But he didn't. Not a word. Not a bit of compassion. And yet, I still found myself thinking about him afterward.

I guess it's true what they say people will always show you their real colors, especially when you've been the one listening, supporting, and being there for them.

When it comes down to me, it often feels like nobody really cares. And yet, I've always been the one who is caring, loving, appreciative, respectful, honest, loyal, and trustworthy. Still, somehow, I'm the one who ends up getting played.

I've worked hard to change my life, to leave my past behind. I took all my mistakes my "dirty laundry" to God and asked Him for forgiveness. That process changed me, but it never stopped me from being supportive and caring toward others.

Even now, a part of me still wishes certain people would come back and apologize for the hurt they caused. Deep down, though, I know that day will never come. It would take a cold day in hell before that happens.

I will admit, I did once receive an apology, and it shocked me. But I accepted it with grace, without an argument. Because at the end of the day, it takes a grown man or a grown woman to recognize when they've done wrong.

It reminds me of that old song: *"Love Don't Live Here Anymore."*

ABOUT THE BOOK

This story will share some heartaches, trauma, and painful memories, along with a few good ones as well. As you read, you may recognize similar experiences from your own past or even your present.

At its core, this story is about a mother who gave some of her children away while keeping others, and how that shaped my search for love and belonging. It is about trying to fill the gaps in my life left by never knowing a mother's love, and about my journey to discover myself while carrying so much pain in my heart.

ABOUT THE AUTHOR